THE LORD IS MY SHEPHERD

THE LORD IS MY SHEPHERD

Psalm 23 and Me

BIBLE PORTALS
BOOK V

TOM GOODMAN

THE "BIBLE PORTALS" BOOK SERIES

This book is part of a series called *Bible Portals: Stepping into the Pages of Scripture.* In the final pages, learn more about the series and discover other volumes in the study set.

Endorsements

"I am excited to see the development of this new series by Tom Goodman. Bringing his commitments to Holy Scripture and his insights gained through four decades of faithful pastoral ministry, Goodman has put together thoughtful and well conceived resources to enable pastors, church staff members, and church leaders in their various teaching ministries in local congregations. These outstanding works focus on key sections of Scripture such as the Beatitudes, the Lord's Prayer, the Fruit of the Spirit, significant Psalms, and other important themes. The volumes are carefully outlined, well written, applicable, and accessible. I am happy to recommend this helpful series." —*David S. Dockery, President and Distinguished Professor of Theology, Southwestern Baptist Theological Seminary*

"Tom Goodman draws from the deep well of the Scriptures and his lifelong journey to understand and apply the wisdom of God for the regular person. He is doing it again with this new series of books called "Bible Portals." In readable, relatable chapters, you will find the insights to set a clear path for your future happiness. Enjoy!" *Tim Hawks, Directional Team, Christ Together Network*

GET A SHOT OF INSPIRATION
IN YOUR INBOX EACH WEEK!

Subscribe to Tom's devotional newsletter, *Winning Ways*. Find it at tomgoodman.substack.com

PSALM 23 AND ME

David Diamond likes word tattoos. Whenever he sees one, he asks about it and posts a photo of the bearer on his Instagram.

Some are the names of loved ones. Others are inspirational quotes. Bible passages show up a lot.

In an article for *The Atlantic*, he reported that one biblical passage has been "a constant" in his photo collection.

Psalm 23.

Sometimes it's just the title inked on the skin. Sometimes it's a phrase from the poem. ("Fear no evil" is a favorite.) He's even met a few people who got the entire psalm etched on their skin in the original Hebrew language.[*]

The phrases of this little poem don't just show up on skin. The lines and images have impacted our culture's novels, films, and songs more than any other biblical passage.

---

[*] David Diamond, "The Words People Write on Their Skin," *The Atlantic*, *https://www.theatlantic.com/ideas/archive/2024/08/photographer-word-tattoos/ 679511/*, accessed 8 May 2025.

Major composers like Bach, Bernstein, and Schubert have set the psalm to music. Queen Elizabeth wanted a seventeenth-century hymn version of it sung in her funeral service —just as she had it sung at her wedding.

Coolio opened his hit song "Gangsta's Paradise" by quoting from it. Megadeth recited the entire composition for the track, "Shadow of Deth," from their album, *The System Has Failed*. The Grateful Dead and Eminem have used some of the lines in their works, too.

You'll also find the verses in many films. *Full Metal Jacket. Titanic. We Were Soldiers. True Grit. Van Helsing. Terminator: Salvation.*

Louisa May Alcott alluded to the psalm in her novel *Little Women*. President George W. Bush recited part of the psalm when he addressed the nation after 9/11.

The poem's images aren't always employed in a positive light. In Pink Floyd's 1977 *Animals* album, the sheep of the psalm are derided as passive and easily led. In U2's song, "Love Rescue Me," the singer curses "thy rod and staff" because "they no longer comfort me." And Clint Eastwood's film, *Pale Rider*, opens with a girl reciting the entire psalm, stopping at the end of each line to complain about how God had failed to fulfill the promises. (Of course, since Eastwood's character mysteriously appears right after her prayer, the viewer can only conclude that God responded to all her troubles, after all.)

So, this little 3,000-year-old biblical poem has attracted widespread attention in our culture. But what do the words and images mean?

Still waters.

The valley of the shadow of death.

My cup overflows.

All the little books in the *Bible Portals* series are designed to bring readers into the world of the Bible by way of "portals." This is my word for biblical passages or images still familiar to people in our culture, even if they've never read the Bible.

Clearly, one of these portals is the Twenty-Third Psalm.

This poem encompasses all of life. Whether you're facing good days, bad days, or your last day, you'll find comfort and challenge in these six little verses. Let's explore the images and phrases that have captured the imagination of so many people across so many generations.

CHAPTER 1

SOMEONE TO WATCH
OVER ME

*"The Lord is my shepherd.
I shall not want."*
Psalm 23:1

Christopher Hitchens once complained, "Everything about Christianity is contained in the pathetic image of 'the flock.'"[*]

To which I heartily say, "Amen."

I know that the famous atheist did not mean it as a compliment. But everything about Christianity truly is contained in that image.

To admit you're a sheep in need of a shepherd is a humbling confession. It implies that we need someone else to give us direction, provision, and rescue.

We don't like this reality. Even some who believe in God prefer to see him as their consultant but not their shepherd.

---

[*] Christopher Hitchens, *Hitch 22: A Memoir* (New York: Hachette Book Group, 2010), 10.

We'd like him to be available when we need a little help in a specific situation, and then leave us alone. But to say with David, "The Lord is my shepherd," we're admitting we need help in every area and at every moment of our lives.

It's only in that admission that life works.

The Apostle Paul wrote, "Therefore I will boast all the more gladly of my weaknesses, so that the power of Christ may rest upon me. For the sake of Christ, then, I am content with weaknesses, insults, hardships, persecutions, and calamities. For when I am weak, then I am strong" (2 Corinthians 12:9-10).

"When I am weak, then I am strong."

As we try to act independently of God's direction and power, we often find ourselves frustrated. But if you're living moment by moment as if you're a sheep under his care and guidance, there's no end to what you can do.

HE KNOWS ME BEST AND LOVES ME MOST

You can find a lot of poetic images of God in the Bible. God is a commander at the head of his angel armies. God is a father. A husband. A mother hen. A strong tower.

In Psalm 23, God is compared to a shepherd.

The very image that filled Hitchens with loathing was precious to the author of the psalm.

King David was at the height of his power and fame when he celebrated his need for God's shepherding care in this psalm.

You probably know that David gained fame even as a boy for killing the giant Goliath with a slingshot. He later took the throne and became Israel's most beloved king. He was not only a warrior and ruler but also a poet. The Old Testament book of Psalms is filled with his compositions.

But before all of that, he took care of his family's sheep. For all his fame and power, what we find in this psalm is a man looking back to his earliest boyhood experiences and saying, "I will always remain a sheep in need of someone to watch over me."

What did he have in mind when he referred to God as his shepherd?

He was saying, "God knows me and loves me."

In David's day, sheep weren't kept behind fences; they had to be taken out to where patches of grass could be found in that dry and rocky terrain. Over time, a shepherd gained a keen knowledge of each member of his flock.

The one that had a stubborn streak.

The one that had grown feeble.

The one about to give birth.

The one nearing death.

In Psalm 23, David was saying, "God knows me as thoroughly as a shepherd knows his sheep."

And how does he use that knowledge of us? He competently cares for those he knows so well. Thus, with God as my shepherd, *I shall not want.* In other words, I have everything I need. Like a flower unfolds from a tight bud, the rest of the psalm unfolds from this first verse.

- *God leads you to green pastures and quiet waters where your soul can be restored.* That's what we'll see when we study verses 2-3 in Chapter 2.

- *God doesn't abandon you when the going gets tough.* In the valley of the shadow of death, he's beside you, protecting you from evil. That's what we'll see when we study verse 4 in Chapter 3.

- *God prepares a table for you where you can safely fellowship with him and be nourished.* That's what we'll see when we study verse 5 in Chapter 4.

- *God surrounds you with his presence here and brings you to his very house hereafter.* That's what we'll see when we study verse 6 in Chapter 5.

The whole psalm is a thorough explanation of what it means for God to be our shepherd. It beautifully illustrates how God guides us through our good days, our bad days, and our last day.

So, God knows us deeply and cares for us thoroughly.

To be fully known and still fully loved. Isn't that our deepest longing?

On the one hand, you can be known and not loved. Sinister forces on the dark web know more about you than you realize. They know you—and they exploit what they know. Likewise, a breakup or a divorce can be so ugly because the one who knows all kinds of intimate things about you can use that knowledge to hurt you.

On the other hand, you can be loved and not known. Some celebrities complain about this. They have hundreds of thousands of adoring fans who want to take selfies with them, but something's missing. Despite all their wealth and fame, they don't feel known by anyone.

You don't have to be a celebrity to feel this way. Sometimes people hide their fears and failures from those they're closest to. They aren't confident that friends or a marriage partner would still love them if they truly knew these things.

To be known and not loved is unsettling, and to be loved and not known is unfulfilling.

When David called God his shepherd, he meant, "Only the Lord can fully know me and still fully love me."

It's good to have friends, it's good to have a marriage partner who loves you, and it's good to have a mentor to guide you. But don't count on anyone to know you and still love you as thoroughly as God can.

Even the strongest earthly relationships can fail us, but not God. In Psalm 27:10 (NIV), we read, "Though my father and mother forsake me, the Lord will receive me." In Isaiah 49:15 (NIV), God said, "Can a mother forget the baby at her breast and have no compassion on the child she has borne? Though she may forget, I will not forget you!"

That's what David was declaring when he said, "The Lord is my shepherd." God is the only one who knows us best and still loves us most.

THE VOICE FROM THE BURNING BUSH

When David wrote, "It is *the Lord* who is my shepherd," what did he mean? He was telling us something specific about this God who wants to be your shepherd.

In Western culture, we're so used to referring to God as "the Lord" that we're no longer stunned by this title.

When translating the Old Testament from the original Hebrew into English, scholars used the generic word "God" to render the generic Hebrew word *El.* But as they worked through the text, whenever they got to the sacred, untranslatable name for God, they used the title "the Lord."

The sacred, untranslatable name?

Maybe you remember the story of Moses. Like David, he had a season where he was a shepherd. You can find this part of his story in chapter 3 of the book of Exodus. One day, out in some remote place with the flock, he marveled at a bush that burned but was not consumed.

He approached it, and a Voice spoke to him from the fire. "Take off your sandals. You're on holy ground." Moses complied. The Voice said, "I want you to lead my people out of Egyptian slavery toward a promised land."

Moses asked, "What should I say when they ask me who sent me to do this?" The Voice replied, "I am the 'I am.' Tell them the Great I Am sent you."

The name is so sacred that, to this day, observant Jews never speak it aloud or write it out. In fact, in Hebrew, only the consonants remain. Without vowels, we can only approximate a pronunciation: The consonants are YHWH, and so we pronounce it "Yahweh" or "Jehovah." Respecting the sacredness and the untranslatable nature of the word, Bible scholars have rendered it in English as "the Lord."*

Here's the point: When David said, "The Lord is my shepherd," he was not speaking about God in some generic way. He wasn't referring to "the Big Guy," or "the Man Upstairs," or whatever other casual way some people speak of God.

To say that *Jehovah* was his shepherd, David was speaking about the God of the burning bush. This is the God who revealed certain things about himself to a certain nation at a certain time in human history. He is the creator. He is the author of the Ten Commandments. He is the one who raises up and brings down nations. He is the one who determines your eternity.

This is the God who relates to us like a shepherd.

---

* Find out more about how God's sacred, untranslatable name has been handled by translators in Jonathan Atkinson's online article, "What Does *yhwh* Mean?" at The Gospel Coalition, https://www.thegospelcoalition.org/article/what-yhwy-mean/, accessed 12 July 2025.

THE LORD WHO IS YOUR SHEPHERD

It's important that we live in the balance of his *title* and his *description*: He is "the Lord" and "my shepherd."

His title reminds us he is the omniscient, omnipresent, omnipotent maker and ruler of the universe. His description as a shepherd reminds us that he graciously accompanies ordinary people like us through all our days.

The Lord is your *shepherd*.

Did you know that Jesus referred to himself by this title and this description?

In John 8, the religious leaders argued with Jesus about his claims, and he said the most audacious thing to them: "Abraham rejoiced at the thought of seeing my day; he saw it and was glad."

His enemies scoffed, "You are not yet fifty years old, and yet you claim to have seen Abraham!" Jesus replied to them, "Very truly I tell you, before Abraham was born, I am!" (John 8:56-58, NIV).

I am.

Where have we seen that before? It was the name God revealed to Moses at the burning bush.

Later, in John 10, Jesus said, "I am the good shepherd.... I and the Father are one" (John 10:14, 30).

Do you know what he was saying? He meant, "When David declared 'The Lord is my shepherd'—well, here I am."

Everything in Psalm 23 was fulfilled by Jesus.

- *In Psalm 23, King David said, "He makes me lie down in green pastures" (verses 2-3).* Perhaps the Apostle John had that in mind when he wrote about how Jesus fed five thousand by miraculously multiplying a few loaves and fish. Jesus said, "'Have the people sit

7

down.'" The Apostle John added, "There was plenty of grass in that place, and they sat down" (John 6:10). He made them "lie down" in green pastures, and he fed them.

- *In Psalm 23, King David said, "Even though I walk through the valley of the shadow of death, I will fear no evil, for you are with me" (verse 4).* The Apostle Paul wrote, "We believe that Jesus died and rose again, and so we believe that God will bring with Jesus those who have fallen asleep in him" (1 Thessalonians 4:14). In other words, even when we walk into death's valley, Jesus will say to us, "Don't be afraid. I've been here before and I know the way out."

- *In Psalm 23, King David said, "You prepare a table before me in the presence of my enemies" (verse 5).* The night before he died on the cross, Jesus prepared a table for his disciples. The city was filled with enemies who would soon arrest him and ensure he was executed. But Jesus took bread and wine and said, "Here we are together in this unhurried, unharried moment. Take these symbols of my sacrifice for you. Eat and be nourished" (1 Corinthians 11:23-25, paraphrased).

- *In Psalm 23, King David said, "I shall dwell in the house of the Lord forever" (verse 6).* Jesus said, "My Father's house has many rooms.... I go and prepare a place for you, [and] I will come back and take you to be with me that you also may be where I am" (John 14:1-3).

When you meet Jesus in the Gospels, everything David declared about God in Psalm 23 is on the nametag stuck on his chest: "Hello, my name is the Good Shepherd."

NOW IS THE TIME

So, when should I commit myself to the Lord as my shepherd? According to the first verse of Psalm 23, the answer is "Now. The Lord *is* my shepherd now."

It takes some of us a long time to appreciate how attentively God has shepherded us. I was struck by what the old patriarch Jacob said in his later years. In Genesis 48:15, he said to his family, "God has been my shepherd all my life to this day."

If you know anything about the story of Jacob, you know he didn't always feel that way. For many years, he thought success in life was up to him. He depended on outwitting others, besting others, and using deception to get his way.

But looking back from the vantage point of old age, he said, "I now see God was leading me, taking care of me, and even protecting me from me! He has been my shepherd all my life to this day."

If you're a Christian, that's a confession you need to make, too. Don't wait until your old age to acknowledge it.

I love how the Heidelberg Catechism begins. Many Christians go to churches that use catechisms. These are educational devices to train and unify their people around essential truths. A catechism is a series of questions with answers that students must memorize and recite back to their teacher. The Heidelberg Catechism was first created and used by Reformed churches in Heidelberg, Germany, in the 1500s.

Even if you know nothing else about it, you may have heard the first question and answer:

- **Question**: "What is your only comfort in life and in death?"

- **Answer**: "That I am not my own, but belong body and soul, in life and in death to my faithful Savior, Jesus Christ."

That's what you declare whenever you recite Psalm 23. *The Lord is my shepherd. I am not my own, but belong body and soul, in life and in death, to my faithful Savior, Jesus Christ.*

Have you made that declaration?

Notice that the first line of this psalm contains the pronoun "my." The Lord is *my* Shepherd.

There has to come a point where you say, "I am his and he is mine." You can't borrow your faith from your parents, your spouse, or other members of the church you attend. You have to decide for yourself to make Jesus your shepherd.

Why not today? David said, "The Lord *is* my Shepherd." He declared it in the present tense.

If some wrote their own version of Psalm 23, the verb would be in the past tense: "The Lord *was* my Shepherd. There was a time I thought I believed, but I grew up, deconstructed my prior belief system, and drifted off."

For others, the verb would be in the future tense: "Perhaps the Lord *will be* my Shepherd. I'm getting close, but I'm still working it out."

You need to say with David, "The Lord *is* my Shepherd."

Christopher Hitchens scorned the idea that we're sheep in need of a shepherd. But what he dismissed as weakness embodies the faith's central comfort: that you are not abandoned to chaos but held by a shepherd's enduring care.

. . .

"DEAR LORD, I NOW KNOW WHAT 'THE LORD' MEANS WHENEVER I call you that. You are the creator, the God of the burning bush, the one who raises up and brings down nations. And you want to be my shepherd! What an awesome thought! The one who knows me best loves me most. Those of us who are believers renew our appreciation of this. Those of us who need to become believers now say it in the present tense like David: The Lord is—is—my shepherd. Amen."

CHAPTER 2

LORD OF THE DANCE

"He makes me lie down in green pastures.
He leads me beside still waters.
He restores my soul.
He leads me in paths of righteousness
for his name's sake."
Psalm 23:2-3

I can't dance.

Really, I've tried. I'm glad there's no video evidence.

But we all need to learn to keep in step with one important rhythm. Life is a sequence of pausing and progressing, pausing and progressing.

If we make life all about just the one or the other, things fall apart.

In verse 2, David compared God to a shepherd who leads us into green pastures beside still waters to restore our souls. But then in verse 3, our divine shepherd leads us into "paths of righteousness."

Fields are for resting. Paths are for walking. God leads us into both in due time.

This is the way ordinary life was meant to be lived.

Do circumstances disrupt this pattern? Of course. We haven't reached the fourth and fifth verses in our study yet. In verse 4, David will describe the dark moments that occasionally come. In verse 5, he will describe the stressful moments that sometimes arise.

At some point in your life, you will need each verse in this poem.

But most of your life will be filled with the ordinary rhythm of pausing and progressing, pausing and progressing.

That is, if you let him lead the dance.

So, let's examine where our shepherd leads us and why he does things this way. Note the two places the word "leads" shows up in the English Standard Version:

Verse 2: "He *leads* me beside still waters"
Verse 3: "He *leads* me in paths of righteousness."

These verses tell us two places the Lord leads us.

BESIDE STILL WATERS

First, he leads us into rest.

I don't know if you could ever find a more refreshing image than the one David painted here. Just read these words out loud and see if a little stress doesn't leave your body:

He makes me lie down in green pastures.
He leads me beside still waters.
He restores my soul.

Where did David come up with this image? I pointed out in the first chapter that David himself had been a shepherd. Growing up as the youngest son in his family, he was assigned to care for the sheep. No matter how powerful or famous he became, he looked back to his earliest boyhood experiences as a shepherd in this psalm. He said, "The Lord does for me what I once did for sheep. He leads me into green pastures beside still waters where I can lie down in contentment until my soul is restored."

Some of us are hard-charging people who never want to stop. Some of us are very dutiful and responsible people who never feel it's okay to stop.

If you aren't careful, you can become the butt of an old joke told in recovery groups: "The main difference between you and God is that God never thinks he's you."

If you think you're some sort of Superman who never needs a break, never needs a time to recharge your batteries and regain your strength, take it from King David himself: you do.

You won't be able to provide everything your family needs from you unless you do that. You won't be able to accomplish all you want at college or your job unless you do that. You won't be able to do what God has called on you to do for your church unless you do that.

So, the Lord leads us into times for rest.

According to the Bible, God provides three regular times for rest: a nightly sleep, a weekly sabbath, and an occasional retreat.

First, a nightly sleep. In Psalm 4:8 (NIV), David said:

In peace I will lie down and sleep,
for you alone, Lord,
make me dwell in safety.

Counselors and psychologists warn that our screens are robbing us of the sleep we need each night. There's a time to turn off the news, turn off the lights, turn off our devices, and sleep.

Second, a weekly sabbath. In the Old Testament, God commanded that everything stop for an entire day once a week. It was so important to him that he made it one of the Ten Commandments (Exodus 20:8). God told us to hit the pause button once a week.

And then, third, an occasional retreat. In the Bible, there were times when God took his people to places where they could withdraw from their responsibilities for a while.

For example, the prophet Elijah hit an emotional wall at one point. We won't go into all the details of why that happened, but in 1 Kings 19, he said, "I've had enough. I quit." What did God do? To start with, God simply fed him and let him sleep.

Jesus issued this call to retreat in the New Testament, as well. At one point, Jesus looked at his exhausted men and said, "Come apart with me to a quiet place and get some rest" (Mark 6:31, paraphrased).

If you do not come apart, you will soon come apart.

(No, that's not original with me.)

I think it's interesting that David said our Shepherd *makes* us lie down.

All the commentaries say that the idea here isn't that a shepherd forces the unwilling sheep to lie down. Rather, a shepherd ensures that all the conditions are met for sheep to feel at ease enough to lie down.

I get that. But I'm still convicted about how proactive the verbs are in verse 2. He *makes* me lie down in green pastures and he *leads* me beside still waters. The Good Shepherd doesn't begrudgingly stop when he finds we can't cut it. He

TOM GOODMAN

doesn't scowl at us while we catch our breath, impatiently tapping his foot until his wimpy followers can continue the journey. No. He knows when we need rest, and he leads us into it.

In one of his books, John Ortberg said, "When it comes to the rest we need to restore our souls, we're like our own little children at bedtime. Kids just don't want to go to bed, no matter how tired they are. So at some point as good parents, we pick them up, carry them into their bedrooms, and make them go to bed."[*]

Then Ortberg asked his readers, "Is it bedtime for your soul?"

A nightly sleep, a weekly sabbath, and an occasional retreat. Are there other ways to rest? Sure. Engaging in a hobby is a form of rest. Participating in a sport is a form of rest. It's good to have those. But in the Bible, the Lord gave us three things. Like a shepherd with his sheep, God leads us into a nightly sleep, a weekly sabbath, and an occasional retreat.

PATHS OF RIGHTEOUSNESS

But now, if some of us have trouble resting, some of us get really good at rest and recreation to the utter neglect of our responsibilities. We occupy our hours with everything but duty.

Video games.

Binge-watching old television shows.

Scrolling social media feeds.

Perfecting our pickleball serve.

---

[*] John Orgberg, *Soul Keeping: Caring for the Most Important Part of You* (Grand Rapids, Michigan : Zondervan, 2014), Kindle Edition, location 2048.

Some of us have to admit that what were once harmless diversions have become escapes. We lose ourselves in distractions to the neglect of our responsibilities. We've disengaged from our family or our schoolwork or our jobs. We don't volunteer at church or in the community.

That's why we need to see the other place where the word "leads" shows up in Psalm 23. Verse 2 says the Good Shepherd *leads* me into green pastures beside still waters, but verse 3 says he also *leads* me into paths of righteousness.

So, these verses tell us two things we must let the Lord lead us to. We have to let him lead us *into* rest and also *onto* the right paths.

Green pastures beside still waters are places to stop, but paths lead somewhere. You get on a path when you want to go beyond where you are now.

Most of our translations call these routes "paths of *righteousness*." Don't think of this only in terms of morality. In the Old Testament, the word "righteousness" was used to describe *wise* actions as well as *moral* actions. Whenever we're engaged in what we're supposed to do, that's a righteous route.

So, for example, the Shepherd leads you away from adultery, but he also leads you to actions that will make your marriage flourish. Or the Shepherd will lead you away from spending your money on sinful things, but he will also lead you to earn and save and spend your money wisely.

God will lead you to be a good parent, to be diligent at school and work, to help your church succeed, to make your world a better place, and so on.

So, we need rest; the Lord leads us into rest. But he also leads us onto the right paths. We need to follow him when he tells us to *pause* and when he tells us to *proceed*.

We all know the people who don't know how to rest, but we've also known those who let rest and recreation deteriorate into an increasing escape from their responsibilities. They get lost in golf or video games or hobbies. As a result, they completely neglect parenting or home management or church work or community volunteering.

The night is for sleeping, but then we wake up.

The sabbath is for rest, but then the week begins.

And in the biblical stories, even the retreats came to an end.

Think of Elijah's story in 1 Kings 19 which I mentioned earlier. He was ready to quit, and God led him to rest and provided him with nourishment for a while. But the story ended with Elijah reengaging in the ministry God had called him to.

I also referenced Mark 6 earlier, where Jesus said to his disciples, "Come away with me for a while." But that retreat didn't last forever. It soon gave way to ministry again.

Life is a rhythm of stopping for rest and walking the right paths. Whenever we get out of that rhythm, things fall apart. It's not good to always work and never rest, or always rest and neglect our responsibilities. Either way, we've lost the beat, the dance falls apart, and *we* fall apart.

FOR HIS NAME'S SAKE

Notice not only *where* our shepherd leads us, but *why*. He leads us into rest and onto the right paths *for his name's sake*.

What that means is, "for the sake of his reputation."

You can drop into almost any section of the Bible and discover how important God's *name* is. The third rule of the Ten Commandments is, "You shall not take the name of the Lord your God in vain" (Exodus 20:7). The first request of the Lord's Prayer is, "Hallowed be thy name" (Matthew 6:9, KJV).

I explain this in greater detail in *How to Talk to God:*

Praying the Lord's Prayer. That's Book 2 in the *Bible Portals* series.[*] God's "name" is a sort of shorthand for his being and character. Even today, when you say someone is ruining your good name, you don't mean that the person is making a mocking rhyme of your name like kids will do on the playground. What you mean is that they are trashing your reputation, reliability, and character.

So, for God to shepherd us for the sake of his name means that God acts in such a way that the universe will see him for who he really is. All creation will recognize him as generous, holy, attentive, reliable, and so on.

This life is not about you. The reason that God does all he does is not because you're awesome but because he is.

There's a scene at the end of *The Hobbit* where Gandalf has to remind Bilbo Baggins: "You don't really suppose, do you, that all your adventures and escapes were managed by mere luck, just for your sole benefit? You are a very fine person, Mr. Baggins, and I am very fond of you; but you are only quite a little fellow in a whole wide world after all!"[†]

It's a lesson we must all learn about our own little lives.

We don't like to hear this. We want to think God saves us because, deep down, he sees something worth saving. Some people might modify that a bit and say that God doesn't save us because we're wonderful now, but he saves us because he knows how wonderful we'll be once we clean up our act.

But where does that leave us when we find out that we're not so wonderful after all?

- What happens when we find out that we're as

---

[*] Tom Goodman, *How to Talk to God: Praying the Lord's Prayer* (Austin: Mainsail Media, 2024).

[†] J.R.R. Tolkien, *The Hobbit* (New York: Ballentine Books, 1966; original copyright 1937), 286-87.

rebellious as the Israelites? They tested and tried God's patience over and over again after he rescued them from Egyptian slavery.

- What happens when we find out we're as cowardly as the apostles? They spent three years with Jesus, and then the night before the cross, they abandoned him.

- What happens when we realize that what Paul wrote in Romans 7 applies to us? "I do not understand what I do," Paul wrote. "For what I want to do I do not do, but what I hate I do.... I have the desire to do what is good, but I cannot carry it out. For I do not do the good I want to do, but the evil I do not want to do—this I keep on doing.... What a wretched man I am! Who will rescue me from this body that is subject to death?" (Romans 7:15-24 NIV.) When you take God's expectations seriously, you are going to draw the same conclusion about your life that Paul did in Romans 7. Then what?

No. You need to base your relationship with God on something a lot more stable than how wonderful you think you are. Salvation is God's invitation into a story that's not about you but about him.

HE LEADETH ME: O BLESSED THOUGHT!

So, verses 2-3 of Psalm 23 tell us that your life with God is a rhythm of *rest* and *right paths*. We rest in him, and we follow him in wise and responsible living. After God leads us like this our entire lives, the whole universe is going to say, "God, you really do live up to your reputation! Seeing how you never gave up on him and how you stuck with her is proof that you really are the most gracious and patient and merciful being there is!"

Back in 1862, the pastor of the First Baptist Church of Philadelphia prepared to preach on Psalm 23. He wrote a song to end the sermon.

Without his knowledge, his wife submitted it for publication. Three years later, Pastor Joseph Henry Gilmore was surprised when he heard his song while visiting the Second Baptist Church of Rochester, New York.

This was the Civil War era, so the song has all the "thees" and "thous" of religious language from that time. It begins:

He leadeth me: O blessed thought!
O words with heavenly comfort fraught!
Whate'er I do, where'er I be,
still 'tis God's hand that leadeth me.

The song goes on to say that God leads him whether his days are bad or good.

Sometimes mid scenes of deepest gloom,
sometimes where Eden's flowers bloom,
by waters calm, o'er troubled sea,
still 'tis God's hand that leadeth me.

In the last stanza, he celebrated that, even in death, he knew God would lead him through.

And when my task on earth is done,
when, by thy grace, the victory's won,

e'en death's cold wave I will not flee,
  since God through Jordan leadeth me.

And thus, the chorus between each stanza is a firm declaration of his trust in wherever God decided to take him:

He leadeth me, he leadeth me;
  by his own hand he leadeth me:
  his faithful follower I would be,
  for by his hand he leadeth me.

God guides us to rest and then to rise with restored strength to fulfill our righteous responsibilities, all for his glory.

"LORD, HOW WE NEED TO LEARN THE RHYTHM OF RESTING AND rising, resting and rising. Some of us need the green pastures beside still waters. We're worn out and wrung out, and we need our very souls restored. Thank you for being a God who recognizes that and provides rest. Some of us have to admit we've sat passive and unengaged for too long, and we sense your call to get going on the right paths once again. And so, help us learn the rhythm of resting and rising—resting from our labors and rising to them again—day after day, season after season. This is how normal life should be lived as we play our part in a story that's much bigger than us, a story that leads to the whole universe praising you for your grace and patience and promise-keeping. Not to us, O Lord, not to us, but to your name be the glory. Amen."

CHAPTER 3

WHO IS WITH YOU IN YOUR
CRISIS?

*"Even though I walk through
the valley of the shadow of death,
I will fear no evil,
for you are with me;
your rod and your staff,
they comfort me."*
Psalm 23:4

How fast can your circumstances change?

In Psalm 23, it only took one verse.

This beloved psalm begins with a comforting image of a shepherd caring for his sheep.

He makes me lie down in green pastures.
He leads me beside still waters.
He restores my soul.

But with the next phrase, the pastoral scene dissolves like chalk art in the rain: *Even though I walk through the valley of the shadow of death....*

In one verse, the green pastures and still waters vanish, and we find ourselves in darkness.

It happens that fast. One phone call. One doctor's visit. One email alert. Suddenly, you've gone from normal living to crisis living.

In verse 4, David vividly described *what* crisis living feels like, *where* God is when we're in crisis, and *how* we must respond.

DEATH VALLEY

David said the crisis times feel like walking through the dark shadow of a deep valley.

He had been a shepherd before becoming a warrior and a king, so he was familiar with leading sheep. David would have recalled the times he had to lead the sheep through low and narrow stretches of the terrain.

These would have been wadis, long and deep gulleys created by decades of rain in the winter. In the summer, these wadis would be dry, and shepherds found that these routes were the straightest shot to get sheep up to the higher grasslands. But while the flock passed through the ravines, there was no green grass or fresh water or sunshine there. The pathways could be a few miles long but no more than 12 feet wide, with tall canyon walls on either side. It was a place of cold shadows and the constant threat of predators.

When we get to verse 4 in this psalm, David said his life wasn't always spent like a sheep in green pastures beside still waters. Sometimes it felt more like he was a sheep following the shepherd through these shadowy, unsettling places.

When you see the word "death" in this verse, you might assume that the verse is about facing a terminal diagnosis. Since the only time most people come across Psalm 23 is at a funeral service, that just reinforces the assumption that the poem is about death.

It is, but it isn't.

David and his generation interpreted life-threatening crises as the long, cold fingers of death stretching out in advance toward the living.

Severe sickness.

Storms that washed away crops.

Rumor of enemy invasion.

A funeral service for a loved one.

David called these moments "the valley of the shadow of death." Not the valley of death, but the valley of the shadow of death.

We walk through the valley of death just once, but we spend our whole lives in the valley of the shadow of death.[*] Long before we're put on hospice, we face many events that remind us that life isn't forever.

Hospitalization.

A friend's funeral.

Wartime troop deployment.

Biopsies.

These are moments in the shadow of death.

So, we all face these seasons in the dark valley. And under-

---

[*] Joseph Sittler, quoted in Cornelius Plantinga, Jr., *Not the Way It's Supposed to Be: A Breviary of Sin* (Grand Rapids Michigan: Eerdmans, 1995), pg. 1. In John Calvin's commentary on Genesis from the 1500s, he wrote, "The misery and evils both of soul and body, with which man is beset so long as he is on earth, are a kind of entrance into death, till death itself entirely absorbs him." Quoted in David Gibson, *The Lord of Psalm 23: Jesus Our Shepherd, Companion, and Host* (Wheaton: Crossway, 2023), 64-65. "In his remarkable work on resurrection in Jewish Scripture, Jon Levenson shows ... how death was understood in ancient poetry. Death was something more like a force that cast its influence (indeed, its 'shadow') even within what we would now call the land of the living." Richard S. Briggs, *The Lord is My Shepherd: Psalm 23 for the Life of the Church* (Grand Rapids, Michigan: Baker, 2021), 94-95.

stand that it's not always because of bad choices. We can find ourselves in miserable circumstances because we've ignored God's will, of course. But even faithful believers find themselves in crisis times that they didn't create. David said it felt like going through a dark and threatening valley.

THE SPINE OF THE PSALM

When we go through these kinds of dark and threatening times, what's often the first complaint we raise? We want to know where God is. We assume that we wouldn't be in crisis if God were present.

That's why David's confident declaration is so important to hear. He didn't demand, "I'm in crisis, so where are you, God?" Instead, he said, "Right here in this crisis, you are with me."

Did you notice in verse 4 that David started talking *to* God and not just *about* God? Up to this point, it's all been "*he* makes me lie down in green pastures ... *he* leads me beside still waters ... *he* restores my soul ... *he* leads me in paths of righteousness."

But when he described life under the shadow of death, he said, "*You*... you are with me."

In tranquil meadows, we're quick to speak *of* God; in treacherous valleys, we're compelled to speak *to* him.

This declaration is not only in the middle of verse 4 but in the middle of the entire poem.

In Western literature, the most dramatic moment is often at the end. That's where we get the big revelation or the moral of the story.

In Hebrew literature, the most dramatic moment is often in the middle. Things lead up to that point, and then the rest of the poem or story teases out the implications of the big revelation in the middle.

So, notice what's in the center of Psalm 23. The poem begins and ends with the covenant name, the sacred name. In the first verse, David said, "*The Lord* is my shepherd." In the last verse, he said, "I shall dwell in the house of *the Lord* forever." Between these two bookends, David declared at the midpoint, "You are with me."

Right in the middle of the *poem,* we find God right in the middle of our *crisis.*

David Gibson called this "the spine of the psalm."*

Anyone with back pain can tell you how important the spine is. Back pain impacts every other body part: hips ... knees ... neck ... shoulders. Physical therapists tell us to take care of our backs.

If the line "you are with me" is the spine of the psalm, you had better take care of it. Meditate on the scriptures about God's character and promises. Sing songs that reinforce these truths. Ask other believers to pray with you that your faith would stay strong. When times get hard, these things will help you maintain your conviction that God is with you.

I like what Kenneth Wilson wrote in one of his books. He told of growing up in an old house in Pittsburgh. At night, it was creaky and shadowy and scary. He said when his father tucked him into bed, "that bed seemed to be at the end of the

---

* The "spine of the psalm is the close, deeply personal relationship between its author, and the person it describes. This is expressed as a 'he – me' relationship in the opening lines, which is close enough, but then most beautifully and seamlessly becomes 'you – me' in the valley of the shadow of death. As [Alec] Motyer says, 'the darker the shadow, the closer to the Lord!'" Gibson, 4. Gibson is quoting from Alec Motyer, *New Bible Commentary* (Leicester, UK: Inter-Varsity Press, 1994), 500.

earth, remote from human habitation, close to unexplained noises and dark secrets."

Sometimes his father read him a story, but inevitably the time came when he turned out the light and shut the door. "I would hear his steps on the stairs, growing fainter and fainter," Wilson remembered. "Then all would be quiet, except for the rattling windows and my cowering imagination."

Once, his father said, "Would you rather I leave the light on and go downstairs, or turn the light out and stay with you for awhile?"

What do you think he decided?

Wilson said he chose "presence with darkness, over absence with light."[*]

That is what we need most in our crisis.

ROD AND STAFF

But what kind of God was with David in the dark valley? In verse 4, he carries a rod and staff.

These were a shepherd's most important instruments in ancient times.

First, a shepherd carried a rod. This was what we would call a club. It was a length of hardwood like a thick baseball bat. Sometimes it had spikes of iron sticking out on the business end. It was a defensive weapon to fend off predators.

David knew that a shepherd had to be ready to defend his sheep. It was a point he raised while begging Saul to let him

---

[*] Kenneth L. Wilson, *Have Faith without Fear* (Harper & Row, 1970), p. 54; quoted in Lloyd Stilley, "Comfort in Times of Crisis," January 1, 2014, https://www.lifeway.com/en/articles/sermon-crisis-lord-shepherd-psalm-23, accessed 3 June 2025.

fight the giant Goliath. When the king objected that he was just a boy, David told the king that, though he was too young to be a soldier, he already had experience as a fighter: "Your servant has been keeping his father's sheep. When a lion or a bear came and carried off a sheep from the flock, I went after it, struck it and rescued the sheep from its mouth. When it turned on me, I seized it by its hair, struck it and killed it" (1 Samuel 17:34-35).

A shepherd needed defensive weapons because sheep don't have any way to defend themselves on their own. On one of his blog posts, Tim Challies wrote:

> Left to themselves, sheep will not and cannot last very long.... Put a sheep in the wild and you've just given nature a snack.... He doesn't have claws, he doesn't have fangs, he doesn't have venom, he doesn't have spines or quills or large talons. He's got nothing to protect himself.... A dog will bark and growl and show his teeth to warn you away. A lion will roar. A rattlesnake will shake his rattle. A cat will arch his back and hiss. The best a sheep can do is baaa.... It is for good reason that no one relies on a guard sheep to keep their property secure. *

David knew how dependent sheep were on the protection of the shepherd. And in Psalm 23, he said, "God, I'm so glad you play that role in my life." He was a valiant warrior and king, but David said, "I face situations that remind me I'm just a sheep in need of a powerful shepherd."

---

* Tim Challais, "Dumb, Directionless, Defenseless," Challais, 26 August 2013, https://www.challies.com/christian-living/dumb-directionless-defenseless/, accessed 3 June 2025.

What do we need protection from when we go through a crisis?

Some might think David expected God to defend him from his circumstances. When sickness or unemployment threatens us, won't God rescue us from that? We praise God when it happens, of course. But some things that accompany the threats are often worse than the threats themselves. Despair. Resentment. Faithlessness. Bad moral choices.

We need protection from these things as much as sheep need protection from predators.

Second, a shepherd carried a staff. If the rod was a club to fight off predators, what was the staff for? It was to manage the sheep under his care. The shepherd could reach out with his staff and nudge the side of a sheep to keep it in line. The shepherd could use it to pull a sheep out of a tight spot.

And so, David was saying, "God, I see you with your rod and staff and I know you're on the job. You've got a rod to protect me from predators, and you've got a staff to protect me from *me*."

THE GLANCE AND THE GAZE

How should we respond to these truths? We must decide what deserves our passing glance and our steady gaze.

Fear *grows* as we gaze at our problems and only glance at God. Fear *goes* as we gaze at God and only glance at our problems.

David determined that his circumstances deserved no more than a glance. He said, "I will not fear." The verb has the sense of a resolution: "I *will* not fear. I am *determined* not to fear."*

But then he expressed where he would fix his steady gaze. He said, "I will take comfort when I see in your hands the rod to protect me and the staff to guide me."

The translation we're using says, "Your rod and staff *comfort* me."

Does that mean giving someone a warm beverage and singing "Soft kitty, warm kitty, little ball of fur"?† Was that what David meant by the word *comfort?*

No. The word in Psalm 23 has the same meaning as it does in the U.S. Constitution. Our nation's founding document defines treason as "giving aid and comfort to the enemy." The word "comfort" in the 1700s meant encouragement, reassurance, and strengthening. That's what David meant in verse 4 when he said to God, "Your rod and staff comfort me."

He was saying, "God, when I see you standing beside me

---

* In his sixteenth-century commentary on the Psalms, John Calvin said of this verse: "David did not mean to say that he was devoid of all fear, but only that he would surmount it.... He says, in the first place, I will fear no evil; but immediately adding the reason of this, he openly acknowledges that he seeks a remedy against his fear in contemplating, and having his eyes fixed on, the staff of his shepherd.... What need would he have had of that consolation, if he had not been disquieted and agitated with fear? It ought, therefore, to be kept in mind, that when David reflected on the adversities which might befall him, he became victorious over fear and temptations, in no other way than by casting himself on the protection of God. This he had also stated before, although a little more obscurely, in these words, For thou art with me. This implies that he had been afflicted with fear. Had not this been the case, for what purpose could he desire the presence of God?" John Calvin, *Commentary on Psalms,* Christian Classics Ethereal Library, https://www.ccel.org/ccel/calvin/calcom08.xxix.i.html, accessed 3 June 2025.

† On the television show, *The Big Bang Theory,* Dr. Shelton Cooper didn't know much about how to relate to people. So, whenever someone was in distress, he just did what his mother did for him as a boy: He made them a hot beverage and offered to sing a nursery rhyme to them.

with the equipment of a shepherd, I know you're on the job. That reality encourages me, reassures me, and strengthens me spiritually to keep going."

When you're in a crisis, it's a great temptation to occupy your mind with all that's going wrong and all that might go wrong. We have to choose to focus on God. Even better, we have to talk directly to him as David did: "God, you are with me, and you are strong to save, and I place my hope in you."

I think it's instructive that David used the words "walk" and "through."

The word "walk" implies that crisis times are usually not brief. When we're in a crisis, it feels like a long, weary slog. David didn't say, "Even though I *run* through this valley," or "Even though I *fly* through this valley." He used the word "walk."

He also used the word "through." It's a valley, not a dead end. To go through something implies that there's another side.

But while we're in it, we have to know what deserves our glance and our gaze. We will not fear if our gaze is on God.

"I'VE BEEN HERE BEFORE"

Now, here's what happens when we turn the Bible's pages and move from the Old Testament to the New Testament.

- David was a warrior king who said, "I need a shepherd" (Psalm 23:1). Jesus was a humble carpenter who said, "I am a shepherd—the good shepherd" (John 10:11).

- David said to King Saul, "When I was a shepherd, I *risked* my life for the sheep" (1 Samuel 17:34-35).

Jesus said, "I *give up* my life for my sheep" (John 10:11).

All we like sheep have gone astray (Isaiah 53:6), but Jesus laid down his life for us. He died on the cross to carry away our sins. Three days later, on a Sunday, he rose again over sin and the grave. Jesus predicted it before it happened. He said, "I lay down my life that I may take it up again. No one takes it from me, but I lay it down of my own accord. I have authority to lay it down, and I have authority to take it up again" (John 10:17-18, NIV).

This is good news because there will come a day when the valley of the *shadow* of death will become the valley of death.

You will die.

Even if your loved ones surround your deathbed, when you take your last breath, you'll go where they cannot accompany you.

But the shepherd is there. Jesus died and rose again. And when he comes to meet us at the moment of our death, we will hear him say, "I've been here before. I know the way through. Here – take my hand."

Life can abruptly shift from peace to crisis. The ultimate crisis is death, but well before that, you'll face numerous circumstances that remind you life is fragile and fleeting. And the closer your day comes to the end, the longer death's shadows stretch toward you. When those times come, be careful what you're glancing at and what you're gazing at.

"GOD, WE LIKE BEING YOUR SHEEP IN THE SUNNY GREEN pastures beside still waters. We'd like things to just stay like that. But even when the path goes through dark valleys, we will keep close to

you. Thank you for protecting us and guiding us when things get scary. And thank you for Jesus, who experienced our life and death. Help us appreciate how his death and resurrection illuminate the promises of Psalm 23. It's in his name we pray. Amen."

CHAPTER 4

THE GENEROUS HOST

*"You prepare a table before me
in the presence of my enemies;
you anoint my head with oil;
my cup overflows."*

Psalm 23:5

The Pacific Crest Trail stretches over twenty-six hundred miles. It will take you about 6 million steps to walk it. Many compare it to summiting Mount Everest.

Hikers are grateful for the unexpected help they find along the way. The Los Angeles *Times* ran an article by Chris Erskine about people who open their homes to the adventurers.*

---

* Chris Erskine, "'Trail angels' help keep Pacific Crest hikers on the path," Los Angeles *Times*, 30 December 2014, https://www.latimes.com/sports/la-sp-c1-trail-angels-20141230-column.html#page=1, accessed 4 June 2025.

They're called "trail angels."

"They reach into their own pockets to provide, food, shelter, medicine and hot showers to hikers. If you insist on leaving money under your pillow, they'll usually donate it toward trail maintenance."

The article focused on Donna Saufley and her husband, who "set up tents and a trailer to handle the spring crush." They host about twelve hundred people a year and don't take any money for it. For her, the payoff is the "river of life that washes up to my shore." Traveling the trail "is humbling," Saufley says. "I compare it to the peeling of an onion. You see people for what they are." She's glad to provide a little respite for them on such a journey.

She and her husband call their home "Hiker Heaven."

David said God provided that kind of respite for him: "You prepare a table before me in the presence of my enemies" (Psalm 23:5).

We know our troubles won't last. God will bring us to victory in this life or certainly in the life to come. But is there any provision for us now, amid the difficult circumstances? In verse 5, we learn that even before the problems get settled, God gives us these wonderful moments that refresh and strengthen.

A TARGET-RICH ENVIRONMENT

Several commentators believe Psalm 23 was written as David fled from a rebellion led by his son. When Absalom led a coup against his father, David chose to flee Jerusalem to avoid bloodshed in the holy city.

We don't know if the Twenty-Third Psalm was written during this stressful time. But we do know that another psalm, Psalm 3, was written about the rebellion. In that poem, David said (Psalm 3:1-5)—

> Lord, how many are my foes!
>> How many rise up against me!
>> Many are saying of me,
>>> "God will not deliver him."
>> But you, Lord, are a shield around me....
>> **_I lie down and sleep;_**
>>> **_I wake again,_**
>> **_because the Lord sustains me._**

So, in both Psalm 3 and 23, David was surrounded by enemies. But in the middle of it all, he said, "God gives me *sleep*" (Psalm 3), and "God gives me *nourishment*" (Psalm 23).

The point of verse 5 is *not* that David fantasized about his enemies having to sit in misery without any food while they watched David feast. No. This isn't a desire for revenge.* In verse 5, David told us what God did for David even as he was surrounded by enemies.

Now, David's enemies were literal, but let's broaden the application of this verse to any threatening circumstances. What we need is a way to be refreshed and strengthened even in the midst of these circumstances.

I mean, it's good to know that there's a vacation or a sabbatical waiting for us after we've solved the problem that's

---

* With fear and trembling, I disagree with one of my favorite authors here. In his book on the Psalms, C.S. Lewis addressed Psalm 23:5 as the "worst of all" the cursing psalms. "The poet's enjoyment of his present prosperity would not be complete unless those horrid Joneses (who used to look down their noses at him) were watching it all and hating it.... The pettiness and vulgarity of it, especially in such surroundings, are hard to endure." *Reflections on the Psalms* (New York: Harcourt Brace Jovanovich, 1958), 21.

currently pestering us. And it's good to know in heaven we won't have any more problems. But what about now, as our worries surround us like enemy soldiers? Does God do anything to help us now? Verse 5 says he does.

Someone joked that the Pentagon refuses to demoralize our troops by saying that they are surrounded or outnumbered. Instead, the commanders are instructed to say they are "operating in a target-rich environment."

Right now, some of us are operating in a target-rich environment when it comes to troubles. We don't have just one big one, but numerous ones.

We're worried about our family.

We're worried about our income.

We're worried about our health.

We're worried about our job.

The fears surround us like David's enemies surrounded him.

Mystery novelist Arthur Somers Roche once explained, "Anxiety is a thin stream of fear trickling through the mind. If encouraged, it cuts a channel into which all other thoughts are drained."[*]

The word "worry" comes from a German word which means "to strangle." Worry strangles us spiritually and emotionally.

That's why Corrie Ten Boom once said, "Worry doesn't empty tomorrow of its sorrow; it empties today of its strength."[†]

To help us keep from worrying about our troubles, God

---

[*] Quoted in Nicole Fellows, "The Story Behind the Worry Wart," Medium, 8 June 2016, https://medium.com/the-life-of-a-worry-wart/the-story-behind-the-worry-wart-97d3af841f3a, accessed 4 June 2025.

[†] Quoted in Robert Jeffress, *Choose Your Attitudes, Change Your Life* (Servant: 1992), 45-46.

wants to be our "trail angel." He invites us in for a nice meal even as we're still on the way.

ALL THE FIXINGS

David said, "You prepare a table for me ... you anoint my head with oil ... my cup overflows."

The poetic scenario David had been using up to this point changes.

As we've seen in our studies of the first four verses of the psalm, David used the scenario of shepherding to help us understand how God cares for us. Because of that, some readers assume that all six verses have to relate to shepherding. As a result, they go to great pains to figure out how a shepherd prepares a table for his sheep to eat on and gives them a cup to drink.

That's not the best way to interpret verse 5. Poets are perfectly capable of using various images to get a point across. In verses 1-4, David compared God to a shepherd; in verse 5, David compared God to a gracious host.

It's really not much of a leap for David to go from God as a shepherd to God as a host. As David Gibson has written, "In the ancient Near East, shepherds were entirely and absolutely responsible for their sheep, and hosts were entirely and absolutely responsible for their guests."*

So, in verses 1-4, you're a sheep and God's your shepherd. In verse 5, you're a human guest and God is your gracious and powerful host.

The table, the oil, and the cup. People of David's day would have recognized all these things as the provisions of a wealthy and generous host.

---

* Gibson, 5.

The Table. The meal David described wasn't a handful of roasted grain he scooped up to eat while darting off. David said God provided respite for him as if he were seated at a table with all the fixings. Metaphorically speaking, he was the honored guest at a leisurely, lavish feast.

The Oil. The anointing oil was a welcome refreshment in a dry and dusty land. Ancient people would have appreciated it as much as we appreciate fragrant moisturizing lotion today. So, David wasn't referring to the sacred oil that was used to ordain priests. Nor was he thinking about the healing oil that was used to soothe wounds. David was referring to the attentive provision of a host that was meant to refresh his guest.

The Cup. At this lavish banquet, David found the wine being poured into his cup until he had to say, "Stop, stop. That's too much. My cup is overflowing!" This was no miserly host.

The phrase entered our culture from the King James Version: "My cup runneth over." There was a hit song in the '60s with that title. It reached number 8 on the Billboard 100 and was nominated for a Grammy. It's just one more instance of how popular Psalm 23 has always been in our culture.

At the Lord's feast, even surrounded by all our stressful situations, we can say God is a gracious host who lavishes his attention on us.

The biblical writers often spoke of God's provision as abundant.

- In Isaiah 55:7, it wasn't enough to promise that God will forgive us—Isaiah said he will *abundantly* pardon.

- In Psalm 130:7, it wasn't enough to promise that

with God there is redemption—the poet said there is *plentiful* redemption.

- In Ephesians 3:8, Paul wrote not just of the riches of Christ—the apostle said there are *unsearchable* riches.

And in Psalm 23, God refreshed David as if he were at a lavish feast. Even as you're surrounded by problems, God will give you abundant reasons for hope and joy and confidence.

Jesus said, "In this world you will have trouble" (John 16:33). But he also said, "These things I have spoken to you that my joy may be in you and that your joy may be full" (John 15:11).

YOUR LEMBAS BREAD

In Psalm 78, the court musician, Asaph, recounted the days of the Exodus. The Israelites wandered forty years in the wilderness, testing and trying God all along the way. In verse 19, he sang—

They spoke against God;
    they said, "Can God really
    spread a table in the wilderness?"

God gave them miraculous manna in response to their complaints, but he was deeply disappointed in their faithlessness.

In Psalm 23, David said to God: "I won't be like them, Lord. I know that you can spread a table in the wilderness. I've seen it! You—*you*—prepare a table before me in the presence of my enemies."

The apostles could have said the same thing. On the night Jesus was betrayed, he prepared a table before his disciples in the presence of their enemies. They were surrounded by adversaries just as King David had been, even in the same city where *David's* enemies had conspired against *him*.

On his last day with them, Jesus sent two of his disciples into Jerusalem to find a certain man and tell him, "'The Teacher says, Where is my guest room, where I may eat the Passover with my disciples?'" Jesus said to his men, "he will show you a large upper room furnished and ready" (Mark 14:12-15). The disciples wanted to prepare for the Passover observance. Jesus let them, but he had already arranged everything.

At the meal, he took the unleavened Passover bread, broke it, and gave it to them, saying, "This is my body, which is given for you. Do this in remembrance of me." Then he distributed the cup of Passover wine and said, "This cup that is poured out for you is the new covenant in my blood" (Mark 14:19-20).

Notice this. Jesus did more than *prepare* the meal. Jesus *is* the meal.

What does this mean? Jesus gives you strength by giving you himself. He died as your substitute; he bore the penalty we deserved for our sins. The God who judges our sins made a way for the sentence to be paid without it coming down on us.

And because his sacrificial death made things right between you and God, all kinds of rich provisions come to us like the courses of a rich man's feast.

Discernment and direction for your decisions.

Hope and peace to replace your anxiety.

Purpose and meaning.

A story to give context to our sufferings.

Whenever we take part in the Lord's Supper, it leads us to conclude the same thing the Apostle Paul concluded: "If God is for us, who can be against us? He who did not spare his own Son but gave him up for us all, how will he not also with him graciously give us all things?" (Romans 8:31-32, NIV.)

This is why we're told to participate in the Lord's Supper regularly as Christians. It symbolizes the way God richly provides all we need.

So, as often as you eat the bread and drink the cup, you proclaim the Lord's death until he comes back (1 Corinthians 11:26). We proclaim it to the world and to each other—but we proclaim it to ourselves, too. We need to constantly remind ourselves of the abundant table Jesus prepared for us.

In Roman Catholicism, the Lord's Supper is sometimes called "viaticum." I think this is interesting because, in ancient Rome, a viaticum was the allowance a dignitary was given for traveling on official trips. It's a Latin word which combines two words: *via* and *tecum,* which together mean, "with you on the way." So, to call the Lord's Supper our viaticum means that it's our provision for our trip through life.

Here's a nerdy detail from *The Lord of the Rings*: In the elven realm of Lothlórien, the fellowship that traveled with the ringbearer was given a bread called *lembas*. That was Professor Tolkien's Elvish word that meant "waybread." It was a special bread that would sustain travelers on long journeys. Tolkien was a practicing Catholic, and in one of his personal letters he said that the *lembas* bread was a symbol of the Communion wafer.*

The Lord's Supper is your Elvish waybread. It's your

---

* J.R.R. Tolkien; Humphrey Carpenter, Christopher Tolkien (eds.), The Letters of J.R.R. Tolkien, Letter 213, (dated 25 October 1958), p. 288.

viaticum for life's journey. Every time you gather at the Lord's table, the Lord himself feeds you with the symbols of his sacrifice for you.

BEAUTIFUL PROGRESSION

So, here's the image from verse 5 of Psalm 23. Even as enemies surrounded David, God refreshed him and strengthened him. We don't have to wait until our problems are solved to experience this. We don't have to wait until we get to heaven to experience this. God can strengthen us and refresh us even as our stressful problems surround us.

There's a beautiful progression in Psalm 23. In verses 1-4, David compared himself to a sheep in the care of a good shepherd. Then, in verse 5, David said, "I'm more than a sheep under the care of a shepherd; I'm the guest of a wealthy host who provides an abundant table to refresh me and strengthen me."

But the progression of Psalm 23 isn't over. Even better than a sheep loved by a good shepherd, and even better than being an honored guest at a rich man's table, you'll one day be a permanent resident in the house of the Great I Am.

That's what we learn in the last line of David's great poem. It's to that promise we now turn.

FATHER, LIKE A TRAIL ANGEL ON THE PACIFIC CREST HIGHWAY, you refresh and strengthen me even before my journey ends. Help me to see that, since you did not spare your own Son but gave him up for us all, I can trust that you will also with him graciously give us all things. Help me be more aware and appreciative of your lavish provision for me! Amen.

CHAPTER 5

THE THING WITH FEATHERS

"Surely goodness and mercy shall follow me
all the days of my life,
and I shall dwell in the house of the Lord forever."

Psalm 23:6

In 2018, the Rubin Museum in New York City mounted an art installation called "A Monument for the Anxious and Hopeful." Visitors were invited to write their anxieties and hopes on cards and display them on a 30-foot-by-15-foot wall.

The public could read the anonymous comments left behind by others as well as submit their own. By the end of the yearlong project, over 50,000 cards were on the wall, a vast mingling of anxieties and hopes, sometimes in response to the same subject.

What would you have posted on that wall?

I suggest that you let the last line of David's beloved psalm be a sieve for any thoughts about the future.

A sieve is a tool for separating wanted particles from unwanted ones. When material is placed upon a mesh strainer, smaller elements pass through it, leaving larger elements behind.

In verse 6, King David said he faced the future confidently because he knew that God's goodness and mercy would accompany him on his sojourn through this life until he could dwell forever in the house of the Lord. If we sieved our thoughts about the future through this conviction, we could separate out our anxieties, leaving only hope.

It's a verse about life *here* and life *hereafter*. Notice the words "all the days of my life" and "forever."

> Surely goodness and mercy
> shall follow me *all the days of my life.*

> I shall dwell in the house of the Lord *forever.*

David was saying, "God, all the days of this life *here*, I trust that your goodness and mercy will follow me." And then he said, "God, in the life to come *hereafter*, I look forward to dwelling in your house forever."

Don't you want to live your life and face your death with that kind of confidence?

WHAT LIFE HERE CAN BECOME FOR YOU

In the first half of verse 6, David said: "Surely goodness and mercy shall follow me all the days of my life."

It's a fitting summary of all the previous verses. Verses 1-3 describe normal living; verse 4 features crisis living; verse 5 spotlights stressful living.

We like verses 1-3. The words are all about green pastures

and right paths. Normal life with God is a rhythm of pausing and progressing. We pause to rest and then get up to do the next right thing. That's normal life with God.

Then, in verse 4, David turned his thoughts from normal living to crisis living. David wrote, "Even though I walk through the valley of the shadow of death, I will fear no evil for you are with me." We go through the valley of death just once, but we often find ourselves in the valley of the shadow of death. David declared that the God who provides for us during the normal days is there for us in times of crisis, too.

And then in verse 5, David said that even in the midst of specific threats, God refreshed and strengthened him: "You prepare a table before me in the presence of my enemies; you anoint my head with oil; my cup overflows." David was grateful that God refreshed and strengthened him even in his unresolved hardships.

We have covered all those verses in the previous chapters of this little book.

Now, as John Calvin put it, "Having recounted the blessings which God had bestowed upon him, he now expresses his undoubted persuasion of the continuance of them to the end of his life."*_David gathered up all he had been declaring about God as his shepherd, and he said, "Surely—definitely, undoubtedly, truly—goodness and mercy shall follow me all the days of my life."

Goodness and mercy. What do those words mean?

Goodness is getting what we *don't* deserve. Mercy is *not* getting what we *do* deserve.†

David was confident that God's goodness and mercy

---

* John Calvin, Commentary on Psalms, Volume 1, https://ccel.org/ccel/calvin/calcom08/calcom08.xxix.ii.html, accessed 11 June 2025.
† Adapted from a line by Colin Smith, in his sermon, "He Loves Me," https://openthebible.org/sermon/he-loves-me/, accessed 9 June 2025.

would *follow* him. The word "follow" doesn't mean they just tag along behind. It's an aggressive word. It means *pursue ... chase after.*

Maybe you've seen sheepdogs keeping a flock in line and moving forward. Ancient Hebrew shepherds like David didn't use sheepdogs, but that's a good way to understand what God's goodness and mercy will do. They chase after us, herding us toward heaven.

Some of us could say that's our salvation story. Even as we ran from him, God pursued us.

That's how Francis Thompson described it in a famous poem published in 1890. He had been an opium addict, and he ran from God deeper and deeper into his addiction. But in the poem, he described how God chased after him. The poem is called "The Hound of Heaven."* Thompson wrote:

> *I fled him, down the nights*
> *   and down the days;*
> *   I fled him, down the arches of the years;*
> *   I fled him, down the labyrinthine ways*
> *Of my own mind—*
> *   and in the mist of tears*
> *   I hid from him...*
> *   from those strong feet that followed, followed after.*
> *But with unhurrying chase,*
> *And unperturbèd pace,*
> *Deliberate speed, majestic instancy,*
> *They beat*

---

* You can read the poem at http://www.houndofheaven.com/poem, accessed 4 June 2025. Thompson capitalized the pronouns in reference to God. In the portions of the poem that I've quoted, I used lower-case spelling for the pronouns to keep it consistent with the rest of this book.

In the poem, Thompson descended deeper in his spiritual rebellion, but he kept hearing the relentless footfalls behind him. Finally, at the end of the poem, Thompson said he heard the voice of his pursuer in a turbulent, rushing sound:

'Ah, fondest, blindest, weakest,
I am he whom thou seekest!'

Some of us could say that's how our salvation began: God sought us when we were lost, and he pursued us even as we ran from his will.

You say, "Oh well, yes, I needed that before I became a Christian. But I'm found now. I'm saved. I'm a sheep in his flock. Since I'm on the path, I shouldn't need him to hound me and herd me." David says, "No. His goodness and mercy will chase you toward heaven until you get there."

At the church where I serve as pastor, I once showed a brief video clip of a sheep getting rescued from a trench. As the clip begins, a sheep is stuck in a narrow trench that must have been dug for underground cabling or piping. A young man gently pulls the back leg of the desperate animal until the sheep is out of the ground and standing unharmed beside the trench. Then the sheep runs away, leaps elegantly into the air and—drops squarely into the same trench twenty yards away!*

That's us. Even after we're saved, we will still have moments where we need saving.

David said, "When I think of how God leads me in the normal times, the crisis times, and the stressful times—I know it for sure now: Within whatever circumstances I'm

---

* Watch the video here: https://youtu.be/NY_dpH_KEMs, accessed 4 June 2025

going to face, God's goodness and mercy will be chasing me straight to heaven."

So, the Shepherd is before me (verses 2-3), beside me (verses 4-5), and behind me (verse 6). With such an escort, what do I have to fear?

Patrick of Ireland expressed the same conviction in his famous fifth-century prayer. It's a confident declaration of being surrounded by the protection of Jesus.

> *Christ with me,*
> > *Christ before me,*
> > *Christ behind me,*
> > *Christ in me,*
> > *Christ beneath me,*
> > *Christ above me,*
> > *Christ on my right,*
> > *Christ on my left,*
> > *Christ when I lie down,*
> > *Christ when I sit down,*
> > *Christ when I arise....*

But that's not the last word of our beloved psalm. When "all the days of my life" are done, there's more.

WHAT LIFE HEREAFTER CAN BECOME FOR YOU

David ended his famous psalm by saying: "I shall dwell in the house of the Lord forever."

Most of Psalm 23 is about what God does for us while we're on the way home. But this closing line is about finally arriving at our heavenly home.

Some Bible teachers insist that the word we translate "forever" should be translated "for length of days," serving as a restatement of the phrase "all the days of my life." They believe David was saying that he would return to the sacred place for worshipping God. He would return and never again leave for as long as he lived.

But the same phrase, "for length of days," was used in Psalm 21:4 to reinforce the phrase, "for ever and ever," and it was used in Psalm 93:5 to parallel the phrase "for endless days." We associate wording like this with unending life.

I think David was thinking about finally arriving at what the Apostle Paul would later call "an eternal house in heaven" (2 Corinthians 5:1, NIV).

In John 14, Jesus himself referred to heaven as "my Father's house," and he promised his followers that he would prepare "a place for you" in that house. When everything is ready, he said, "I will come back and take you to be with me."

Earlier, I recommended we use the last line of Psalm 23 to sieve our thoughts about the future. Someone might think, "I can see how thoughts of heaven can be a comfort to those facing terminal illness, but how can the assurance of forever dwelling in God's house help us with anxieties about this life? I'm unemployed and I need a job now. I'm lonely and I want a partner now. How does the promise of heaven help with any of that?"

But think about this. In an advice column for the New York *Times*, Elizabeth W. Dunn and Michael Norton said that "research shows that people frequently experience a happiness boost in the weeks before their vacation. Stuck in an office cubicle, the anticipation of the beach is almost as enjoyable as the beach itself. The French — those masters of pleasure — even have a word that helps capture the thrill of anticipating the future: réjouir."*

---

* Elizabeth W. Dunn and Michael Norton, "Happier Spending,"New York

They're right. When you're in college or on a business trip, doesn't it make it more bearable if you know that someone's getting ready for your return home?

The college semester's hard, but when it's over, you know your mom's going to cook your favorite meal.

The business trip is frustrating, but soon you'll hear the excited greeting from your small children, or you'll see the wagging tail of your dog.

There's nothing like the feeling of being *wanted*. That's how thoughts of heaven can help you deal with earthly frustrations.*

Rick Ezell told a story that anyone who's been the father of a small child can identify with. A father announced to his son that he would take the boy fishing for the first time on Saturday. On Friday night, the child was so wired that he couldn't sleep. He tossed and turned. Finally he went into his parents' bedroom and woke his father.

"Daddy," he said, "I can't sleep. I'm too excited."

His father replied, "Well, son, I'm sure you are, and it's going to be a great day. But it won't be great if we don't get some sleep. So, get back in your bed, and let's have a good night's rest."

"I'll try," the boy said, but before he left the room, the little voice piped up again.

"Daddy."

"What now, son?"

"I ... I just want to thank you for tomorrow."†

Times, 22 June 2013, https://www.nytimes.com/2013/06/23/opinion/sunday/happier-spending.html, accessed 12 June 2025.

* For more information about what Christians believe about heaven, check out Chapter 21 of my book *The Anchor Course: Exploring Christianity Together*, entitled, "What is Heaven Like"? pages 195-203.

† Adapted from Rick Ezell, "The Lamb Who Became a Shepherd - Revela-

We should thank God for tomorrow. The thought of heaven is not escapism. We still have to solve or endure whatever we're facing here. But we can bear it knowing that one day we'll dwell in the house of the Lord forever.

HOPE IS A GOOD THING

The American poet, Emily Dickinson called hope, "the thing with feathers" that "perches in the soul" and never stops singing "the tune without the words."*

A tune without the words. What did she mean by that?

I think she meant that hope is more of a mindset than a conclusion built from a defensible argument. Hope is more than just a wish that the medical test will come out right, or that the rumors of layoffs will not involve you, or that the car won't break down in the middle of the night.

Hope transcends the immediate circumstances in confidence that in all things God works for the good of those who love him (Romans 8:28). Wherever life's path takes us, his goodness and mercy will be right on our heels, herding us all the way home to heaven.

In Stephen King's 1982 novella, *Rita Hayworth and The Shawshank Redemption*, an inmate named Red recounted his experience with Andy Dufresne.† "Andy was the part of me they could never lock up," Red said of his remarkable friend. Though unjustly convicted and sentenced to a lifetime of

---

tion 7," Lifeway, 1 January 2014, https://www.lifeway.com/en/articles/sermon-lamb-who-became-a-shepherd-revelation-7, accessed 11 June 2025.

* Emily Dickinson, "'Hope' is the thing with feathers,' Poetry Foundation, https://www.poetryfoundation.org/poems/42889/hope-is-the-thing-with-feathers-314, accessed 11 June 2025.

† The quotes from King's novel come from the ebook version, so I have no page numbers to reference.

imprisonment, Andy refused to resign himself to his circumstances. Finally, Andy fled from terrible injustice in a magnificently planned breakout.

Years later, Red got his long-sought parole, but he had trouble adjusting to life on the outside. He even thought about committing some crime to get himself back into the structure and predictability of prison life.

That's when he remembered a conversation that he and Andy once had in the prison yard. Andy had told Red about a town that had a certain tree in a certain hay field. There, under a certain rock, he had buried a certain tin can.

Curious now, Red searched for the spot. He found the tin can. Inside was an envelope with his name on it. The envelope contained money and a note. The note was an invitation to join Andy at the fishing village he had escaped to in Mexico.

"Remember that hope is a good thing, Red," Andy had written his friend. "Maybe the best of things. And no good thing ever dies."

This news left Red with a choice between two options: "Get busy living or get busy dying."

The book ends with Red's determination to go in search of Andy's fishing village: "I hope Andy is down there. I hope I can make it across the border. I hope to see my friend and shake his hand. I hope the Pacific is as blue as it has been in my dreams. I hope."

Those two words were how Stephen King ended the novella.

Decide to sift your thoughts about the future through the sieve of this last line of David's beloved psalm. This kind of hope will help you get busy living.

. . .

LORD, I'M SURROUNDED BY YOUR WATCHCARE! AHEAD, I SEE you leading me and all your flock like a shepherd. Behind, I see your "sheepdogs," Goodness and Mercy, herding me homeward. Because of this, I'm confident I will arrive safely at the place you've prepared for me in eternity. To all of this I say, "Thank you!" I'm yours, Lord, here and hereafter! Amen.

"A RULER WHO WILL SHEPHERD MY PEOPLE"

D id you know that Christmas celebrates the birth of the shepherd described in Psalm 23?

That may take some explaining.

Psalm 23 may be the most familiar place where God is compared to a shepherd, but biblical writers often described God in this way. In fact, God *himself* took that title in Ezekiel 34. Some of the imagery in Ezekiel 34 sounds very much like Psalm 23:

> "I myself will search for my flock and look for them. As a shepherd looks for his sheep on the day he is among his scattered flock, so I will look for my flock. I will rescue them from all the places where they have been scattered on a day of clouds and total darkness.... I will tend them in good pasture, and their grazing place will be on Israel's lofty mountains. There they will lie down in a good grazing place; they will feed in rich pasture on the mountains of Israel.... I will seek the lost, bring back the strays, bandage the injured, and strengthen the weak.... I will save my flock....

And then God added, "I will give them a king like my servant David to be their one shepherd, and he will take care of them" (Ezekiel 34:23).

Did you catch that? God said he would personally shepherd the flock through one who would come from the line of David.

Ezekiel 34 is a prophecy of the Messiah.

Centuries after Ezekiel, when the Romans occupied Judea, strange Magi came from the East to Herod's court. They asked, "Where is the one who has been born king of the Jews? We saw his star when it rose and have come to worship him" (Matthew 2:2). Herod asked his religious scholars where the Messiah was to be born, and they said (Matthew 2:5-6), "In Bethlehem in Judea ... for this is what the prophet has written:

'But you, Bethlehem, in the land of Judah,
    are by no means least
    among the rulers of Judah;
    for out of you will come *a ruler*
    who will shepherd my people Israel.'"

The Magi went to Bethlehem and found the baby king and presented him with gifts of gold, frankincense and myrrh.

Does that sound like the Christmas story? It is! The Christmas story is about the birth of the shepherd described in Psalm 23 and prophesied in Ezekiel 34.

But if the Christmas story is about the birth of the shepherd, the Easter story is about the death and resurrection of that same shepherd.

In John 10, Jesus tried to prepare his disciples for this. He said (verses 11-28): "I am the good shepherd." He did not say, "I am *a* shepherd." No, but he said, "I am *the* good shepherd."

Jesus took all those references to God in the Old Testament—Ezekiel 34, Psalm 23, and so on—he took them all as descriptions of himself, and he said, "Here I am, the promised shepherd, living among you."

But in John 10, immediately after claiming to be the good shepherd, he defined what it meant to be the good shepherd. He said, "The good shepherd lays down his life for the sheep."

And then he said something that must have left everyone scratching their heads in confusion. He said, "I lay down my life—only to take it up again" (John 10:17).

What was he doing? He was predicting Easter! He was predicting his death and resurrection. When Jesus died, it was as our substitute. In Isaiah 53:5-6, we read—

> He was pierced for our transgressions,
>   he was crushed for our iniquities;
>   the punishment that brought us
>   peace was on him,
>   and by his wounds we are healed.
> **6** We all, ***like sheep***, have gone astray,
>   each of us has turned to our own way;
>   and the Lord has laid on him
>   the iniquity of us all.

But as we know from the Easter story, he was raised to resurrection life—a resurrection life that he now offers to us. After saying, "I lay down my life only to take it up again," he said (John 10:28), "I give them eternal life, and they shall never perish; no one will snatch them out of my hand."

So, his crucifixion on a Friday broke the hold that sin has over us, and his resurrection on a Sunday broke the hold that death has over us. Our shepherd was *gracious* enough to lay down his life to bear away our sins. And our shepherd was *powerful* enough to rise in victory over death and give his eternal life to us. Jesus is the prophesied ruler destined to shepherd the people of God.

This image of Jesus as our Good Shepherd requires a response of humility and joy.

First, the image says something about us, which we must humbly accept. On our own, we're defenseless and directionless. We may have an alarm system for our homes, train in martial arts, and keep a pistol in our nightstand. But against the real enemies of our soul, we're helpless.

Second, the image says something about Jesus, which we must joyfully accept. He is powerful enough and interested enough to guard our souls against any and all threats.

So, how do you become one of Christ's sheep? Jesus said, "My sheep hear my voice...and they follow me" (John 10:27).

Hear and follow.

Of course, we shouldn't expect to hear an audible voice. I remember a pastor's reply to a reporter some years ago. When the pastor said God had called him to make a certain decision, the reporter asked, "Audibly?" The pastor said, "No, louder than that."

Likewise, if you find a desire in your heart for this Shepherd, that's his invitation to you. When you hear his call— louder than audibly—follow him.

Jesus is the Good Shepherd described in Psalm 23, who lovingly guides, provides for, and protects his flock. He calls us to trust in his care, follow his lead, and walk in the peace and righteousness of his eternal presence.

PLEASE LEAVE A REVIEW!

Help me get the word out about this book! Just one or two sentences from the online bookstore or review site of your choosing will make a big difference!

ABOUT THE SERIES

The book you've been reading is part of a series of studies called *Bible Portals: Stepping into the Pages of Scripture*.

In the short books that make up this series, we'll look into passages like the Lord's Prayer, the Twenty-Third Psalm, the Beatitudes, the Armor of God, the Fruit of the Spirit, and others.

I call these *portals*.

Some of our favorite stories involve portals to other worlds or other eras. The characters step through the entry point on purpose or fall into it by accident. Either way, they discover a strange new world on the other side.

- Alice tumbles down the rabbit hole into Wonderland.

- Harry Potter discovers a whole new world on the other side of Platform 9¾ in London's King's Cross Station.

- An Iowa man hears a voice saying, "If you build it, they will come," and he constructs a baseball diamond in his cornfield that becomes a portal for baseball greats.

- Jack Skellington finds the Holiday Doors in the Hinterland and falls through one of them into Christmas Town, singing, "What's this? What's this?"

Eden Arielle Gordon explained why we love stories about mysterious entry points:

> Portals promise transcendence. They promise that there's something more, perhaps a grand design or some form of discernible meaning. We'd all love to know if there's something else out there in the starry night, as maybe that something would give us clarity as to why we're here on Earth at all.[1]

I've discovered some portals into the world of the Bible. Even if we've never read the Bible, we're familiar with certain passages. We quote them at funerals, print them on wedding programs, or recite them at recovery meetings.

Stand in proximity to these entry points for long and you may find yourself whisked into a place very different than your familiar life. It's a sprawling world of flawed heroes and sinister enemies, soaring poetry and pithy advice, prophetic warnings and hearty encouragement.

I hope you find your way into this world. As a Bible teacher for over forty years, I've seen profound changes in the lives of those who situate their little stories in the Big Story told in the Bible.

To see the other books in this growing collection, go to the section of this book called "Also by Tom Goodman."

I'm hoping that these will serve as entry points for you into a lifetime love of the Bible.

———————————————

1. Eden Arielle Gordon, "Portals to Other Worlds: Where Stonehenge, Harry Potter, and Dark Matter Meet," Magellan, 3 November 2019, https://tinyurl.com/2dm74oes, accessed 20 December 2023.

GROUP DISCUSSION GUIDE

Coming Soon!

You'll soon be able to download a free copy of the Group Discussion Guide for all the books in the *Bible Portals* series.

To find out when this will be available, subscribe to Tom's devotional newsletter, *Winning Ways*. Find it at

tomgoodman.substack.com

ABOUT THE AUTHOR

For over forty years Tom Goodman has discussed faith with believers and nonbelievers while serving as a pastor in Louisiana, the Cayman Islands, and Texas. He is a graduate of Baylor University and Southwestern Seminary in Texas, with a doctorate from New Orleans Seminary. He and his wife, Diane, have two adult sons. He enjoys scuba diving, fly fishing, and puttering around his woodworking shop.

Subscribe to Tom's devotional newsletter, *Winning Ways*. Find it at tomgoodman.substack.com

ALSO BY TOM GOODMAN

Find these other Books in the "Bible Portals" Series

Book One:

The Pursuit of Happiness: Learning from the Beatitudes

Book Two:

How to Talk to God: Praying the Lord's Prayer

Book Three:

Suit Up! Wearing the Armor of God

Book Four:

Nine Noble Virtues: Cultivating the Fruit of the Spirit

Book Five:

The Lord is My Shepherd: Psalm 23 and Me

Other Nonfiction Titles by Tom Goodman

The Anchor Course: Exploring Christianity Together

Repeat the Sounding Joy: The Four Christmas Carols of Luke's Gospel

Winning Ways: Inspiration for Uncommon Living

Fiction by Thomas Goodman

The Last Man: A Novel of the 1927 Santa Claus Bank Robbery

www.ingramcontent.com/pod-product-compliance
Lightning Source LLC
Chambersburg PA
CBHW060347050426

42449CB00011B/2862